How to increase
Sales
using YouTube.

Claretta T. Pam

Claretta T. Pam

How to increase sales using YouTube

Claretta T. Pam

How to increase sales
using YouTube.

Entrepreneurial Universe
Series (Volume 5)

Help Us Keep This Guide Up to Date

Every effort has been made by the author and editors to make this guide as accurate and useful as possible. However, many changes can occur after a guide is published.
We would like to hear from you concerning your experiences with this guide and how you feel it could be improved and be kept up to date. While we may not be able to respond to all comments and suggestions, we'll take all correspondence to heart and make certain to share them with the author. Please send your comments and suggestions to the following address:

Innovative Publishers Inc.
Double Click Press
Book ID #4705119
PO Box 300446
Boston, MA 02130

or you may email us at corrections@innovative-publishers.com

Claretta T. Pam

Cover art and design provided by
Taylor Pam – Fine Art LLC

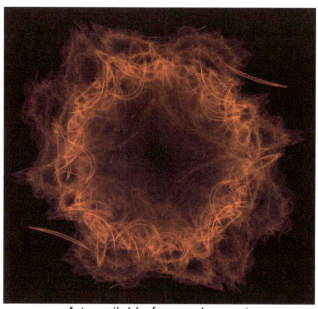

Art available for purchase at
http://taylorpam.artistwebsites.com/featured/fractal-139-taylor-pam.html

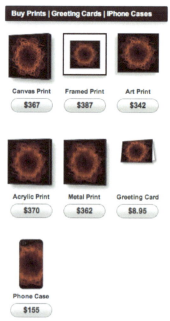

How to increase sales using YouTube

Copyright © 2014 by Claretta Pam

Innovative Publishers, Inc. & Double Click Press and colophon are trademarks of Open Nebula LLC, Intellectual Property Series.

Published and printed in the United States by
Innovative Publishers, Inc., Boston, Massachusetts

Innovative Publishers

Double Click Press

Claretta T. Pam

ISBN-10: 1-4913-2359-0   ISBN-13: 978-1-4913-2359-5 Paperback
ISBN-10: 1-4913-2364-7   ISBN-13: 978-1-4913-2364-9 Hardback
ISBN-10: 1-4913-2369-8   ISBN-13: 978-1-4913-2369-4 Kindle
ISBN-10: 1-4913-2374-4   ISBN-13: 978-1-4913-2374-8 iBook
ISBN-10: 1-4913-2384-1   ISBN-13: 978-1-4913-2384-7 Nook
ISBN-10: 1-4913-2379-5   ISBN-13: 978-1-4913-2379-3 AudioBook

Library of Congress Cataloging-in-Publication Data

Pam, Claretta T., 1969-
   How to increase sales using YouTube / Claretta T. Pam.
        pages cm -- (Entrepreneurial universe series ; 5)
   Includes bibliographical references and index.
    ISBN 978-1-4913-2359-5 (pbk. : alk. paper) -- ISBN 978-1-
4913-2364-9 (hb : alk.
paper) -- ISBN 978-1-4913-2369-4 (ebook) -- ISBN 978-1-
4913-2374-8 (ebook) --
ISBN 978-1-4913-2384-7 (ebook) -- ISBN 978-1-4913-2379-3
(audio book)
   1. Electronic commerce. 2. Web site development. 3.
YouTube (Electronic
resource) I. Title.
   HF5548.32.P356 2014
   658.8'72--dc23

2014014537

10 9 8 7 6 5 4 3 2 1   14 15 16 17 18

An interpretation of the printing code: is the number of the books printing. The rightmost number of the
second series of numbers is the year of the books printing. For example, a printing code of 1–14 shows that
the first printing occurred in 2014.

First edition. June 2014

For general information on our other products and services or for technical support, please contact our technical support within the United States at admin@innovative-publishers.com online at http://innovative-publishers.com.

Most Innovative Publishers Inc. books are available at special quantity discounts for bulk purchases first sales promotions, premiums, fundraising, or educational use. Special books, or book excerpts, can be created to fit specific needs. For details, email info@innovative-publishers.com.

Titles Forthcoming:

How to make money using Facebook
How to make money using LinkedIn
How to make money using Pinterest
How to make money using Twitter

DEDICATION

To the entrepreneur that meets the challenge to follow their dreams.

Table of Contents

ACKNOWLEDGMENTS

CHAPTER 1

Getting Started

What is YouTube All About?

The internet experience has changed completely because of the plethora of music, videos, movies and other digital media that has become available to everyone at the click of a button. At the epicentre of all this, is YouTube.

YouTube is a video-sharing website, which has become the third most visited website on the internet, after the search engine Google and the massive social

networking site, Facebook. Essentially,

The creators of YouTube: (from left to right) Steve Chen, Chad Hurley and Jawed Karim

YouTube allows internet users to upload videos, which can then be watched by anyone who visits the website. In recent times, the popularity of YouTube has risen exponentially, and media corporations, music artists, and social gurus have begun uploading videos on the website in order to boost their popularity.

YouTube was created on February 14, 2005. The people responsible for its creation were Chad Hurley, Steve Chen and Jawed Karim, who were all employees of PayPal. Their goal was to create a website where people could upload, share and view videos.

After February 14, 2005, YouTube continued to develop throughout the year. The first video was uploaded in April. It was called 'Me at the zoo', and it showed Jawed Karim walking around the San Diego Zoo in a video clip that lasted only 19 seconds. In May, the creators gave the public a preview of YouTube and in November, a venture firm called Sequoia Capital invested $3.5 million in the website. In 2006, another $8 million was invested, as the website continued to gain popularity.

During 2006, YouTube experienced a surge in its growth and became one of the most rapidly growing websites on the internet. On average there were 60,000 new videos being uploaded every day during the month of July and over 100 million daily views. The total data usage of YouTube users was recorded at that time as approximately 8 terabytes per day. At the time, the popularity of MySpace was also booming, but YouTube surged ahead in popularity.

Some sources recorded an average of nearly 20 million visitors per month during the summer of 2006. Of those, approximately 45% were female and 55% were male. Children in the age group of 12 to 17 years were the most frequent visitors of the website. During that same year, YouTube and NBC entered into a marketing and advertisement partnership. In October 2006, Google purchased YouTube stocks worth approximately $1.65 billion after YouTube entered into agreements with media companies, in an attempt to avoid violation of copyright infringement laws.

Time magazine named YouTube users the 'Person of the year' in 2006 for making the website the sensation that it had become. The Wall Street Journal and the New York Times also recognized the corporate importance of YouTube that same year and it was named the ninth Best Buy Product in 2006.

Since 2006, YouTube has shown no signs of slowing down its growth. In 2007, the YouTube Awards were started, which aimed at recognizing the best YouTube videos uploaded. The winners were decided by the results of the votes of the entire YouTube community. Two major developments came about in July 2007 and November 2008, when YouTube collaborated with CNN and produced televised presidential debates in the U.S., where the candidates were asked questions submitted by YouTube users.

Through 2009 and 2010, YouTube grew even more in terms of user base and popularity, and gained acclaim from the world over. In 2010, market research showed that YouTube was the largest provider of internet videos in the United States, holding a share of approximately 43% and over 14 billion video views during May of that year.

In 2011, the social networking site Google+ was integrated with YouTube and the Google Chrome internet browser, which allowed users to use these applications more seamlessly. In 2012, YouTube streamed the U.S presidential debate live in partnership with ABC.

Today, YouTube is the third most visited website on the internet and users of the website record over 2 billion video views each day. It has become so much more than what its original intended purpose had dictated and it has forever transformed the internet into more than just an information gathering resource.

CHAPTER 2

Making Your YouTube Account

Although YouTube allows you to view videos without registering, as well as enjoy the full array of features the website has to offer such as being able to upload videos and share them, you need to create an account for yourself to enjoy other features. You will be able to comment on, and rate, videos uploaded by other users. In this chapter, we will present a systematic method on how to create a YouTube account.

Step 1: Visit the YouTube Webpage

In the previous chapter, we talked about how, in 2006, Google bought the majority of YouTube stocks and therefore it now owns the website. Furthermore, in an attempt to harmonize the YouTube experience for individuals who currently have Gmail accounts, Google has synchronized Gmail and Google+ with YouTube.

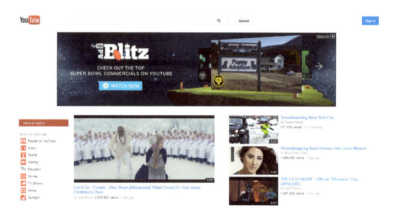

Step 1: Visit YouTube.com

Therefore, when attempting to create an account on YouTube, you will also be creating an account for yourself on Gmail and Google+. Your Gmail username will be:

(YouTube username)@gmail.com or a business email if you have several

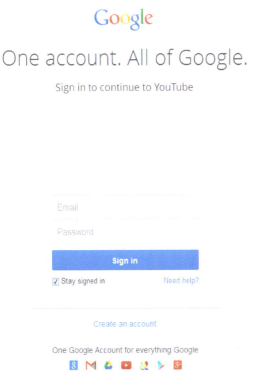

accounts.

This username will also be your identity on Google's social networking site, Google+, which is very similar to Facebook and MySpace. If you do not want a Google+ account, you will have the option of deleting it after your YouTube account is created. Note that your activity on YouTube will be separate from your activity on Gmail or Google+.

Step 2: The Sign In window for YouTube.

Step 2: Sign In

After you visit the YouTube homepage, you will see a small, blue colored button at the top right hand corner of the screen, which reads 'Sign In'. Click on this button and you will be led to a new window.

This is the window shown on the right and will read 'One account. All of Google.' It is clear from this that only one account will give you seamless access to the features of all of Google's sister applications.

5

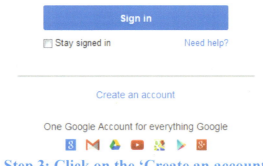

Step 3: Click on the 'Create an account' button

Step 3: Create an Account

If you already have a Google account, then you will simply fill in your details in the two text fields. However, chances are that if you are new to YouTube, you probably will not have an account, in which case you should click on the 'Create an account' button near the bottom of the screen. This will then direct you to the next screen, where you will be asked to fill in your details in order to create a YouTube/Gmail/Google+ account.

Step 4: Fill in the Relevant Details

In this step, you will be asked to provide details which will be used to create your YouTube account. Note that this account will also be your Gmail and Google+ account, and the details required are nearly the same as those required when you create an email address with any

email service provider such as Yahoo! or Hotmail.

You will be asked for your name, a username, password combination of

Step 4: Provide the necessary details for your Google account

your choice, as well as your birthday, gender and phone number. Once you have supplied these, you need to agree to their terms and conditions as well as their privacy policy. Once that is done, your account will have been created. Sometimes, your phone number will be used as a verification code, in order for Google to authenticate that you are not a machine or bot, trying to create a fake account.

Step 5: Your Appearance on YouTube

Your initial account on YouTube will have the default profile picture, as shown below. You will, of course, be able to add a new picture to the account and personalize it in a lot of ways.

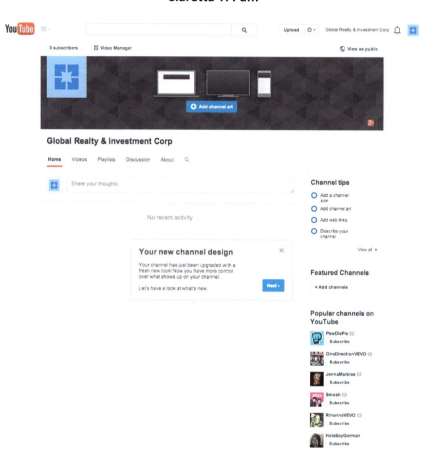

How to Set-up a YouTube Channel

Once you have set-up your account, you will see that if you visit your homepage, it will seem empty. The idea is that you should be able to personalize your own homepage according to the videos and YouTube members you like.

A channel is essentially your homepage on YouTube. It is provided to you by YouTube after you become a member. Anyone who visits your channel will be able to see your profile picture, any details that you have entered and made public, and videos which you have uploaded, shared and commented on. The layout of your channel will also allow you (and others) to see members to whom you have subscribed, your favorite videos, and subscribers who are your friends.

You can visit other member's channels simply by searching for his or her username. As with your channel, you will be able to see the other person's activity on his/her channel. You will be able to see the members to whom they are subscribed and their favorite videos, as well. Thus, with the channel feature, YouTube has also developed a social networking aspect, rather than simply a video uploading and viewing database.

You can customize the look of your account according to your own preferences. You can change the theme of your channel, as well as the background color. YouTube offers several themes which you can use, or you could design your own using hexadecimal color values. You can also control which of your details are visible to the public.

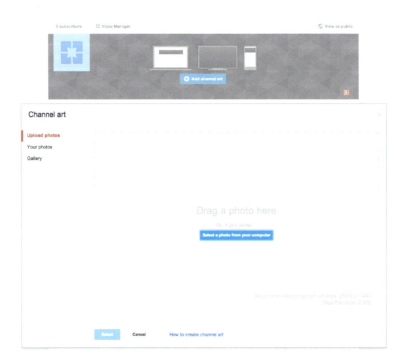

Now, we will take a brief look at how to set-up your channel on YouTube, after you have created your profile/account.

Step 1: Click on the Arrow Next to Your Profile Picture

After you have created your YouTube account, you will see your profile picture in the top right-hand corner of the screen. Note that you have the option to change this picture, if you want to. Click on the box and Click on the small downward pointing arrow next to the picture and a task bar will unfold downwards.

Step 2: Click on the 'My Channel' Button in the Task Bar

When the taskbar unfolds, you will see several options in it. It will contain videos which you have marked as 'Favorites', 'Watch Later', and those which you 'Like'. You will also see your playlist, if you have created one.

However, to the right of all of these, you will see a button which says 'My Channel'. Click on this button and it will lead you to your channel. Again, the appearance of your channel will be very empty and dull at first, so feel free to add your favorite videos to it.

Step 3: Customize Your Channel

Essentially, you have set-up your channel now, but you need to start adding things to it if you really want to enjoy YouTube. On the right-hand side, you will see channel tips. One allows you to add a description to your channel and the others allow you to change the look of your channel. Take this as your chance to be creative and give your channel a personalized touch.

Channel tips

O Add a channel icon

O Add channel art

O Add web links

O Describe your channel

View all »

Below that, the next box will show the channels which are your favorites, FEATURED CHANNELS and another one just below that will give you some suggestions on the current popular channels on YouTube, which you may want to subscribe to, just to get yourself started and add some activity to your channel.

On the left hand side, you have the options of seeing which channels you are already subscribed to, your playlists and your history. You will also see a button which says 'Social'. Clicking on this will take you to a page where you see the latest activity from people whom you have already added on Google+. It will show their recent posts, video comments, likes and shares.

So, use your YouTube channel to its full extent, if you really want the complete experience. Upload your own videos and wait for them to grow in popularity. People will comment on them and like them. Others will subscribe to your channel. Watch videos and comment on them. Add them to your channel if you like them and subscribe to people who upload videos you really like.

Familiarizing Yourself with the Features

YouTube offers users a number of features that allow them to truly enjoy uploading, viewing and sharing videos. In this chapter, we will look at some of the major features, which YouTube offers.

Monetization

This feature allows you, as a YouTube user, to make money through videos that you upload. In order to do this, YouTube signs you up to its Partnership Program. If you meet the criteria to become a YouTube Partner, YouTube will begin showing advertisements on your videos. Since the website charges advertisers for this, you will also be getting a certain percentage of the profit.

Uploading Longer Videos

Initially, you will only be allowed to upload videos that are a maximum of 15 minutes in length. However, you get the option of increasing this limit simply by going into your upload settings. You may need to verify your account using your phone number when you attempt to do so. If you have a good browser, you can upload files that are greater than 20GB.

External Annotation

This lets you add annotation to your videos, in order to make them more interactive. You can layer text, add links and hotspots to your videos. This will make them more informative and interesting for your viewers. Of course, you can change the type of annotation, the text style, font and colors, the timing and even add links to other web pages in the annotation.

Video Thumbnails

This feature allows you to add a thumbnail to your videos. Viewers will be able to see a small picture of the video content by looking at the thumbnail. When you are finished uploading the video, you will be able to select one of three options of the snapshots, which YouTube automatically generates. If you have a verified account, you will get the option to select a custom thumbnail for your video.

Paid Subscriptions

If you have enabled the paid subscription option for your account, you will be able to charge viewers and subscribers a subscription fee in order for them to watch videos on your channel. There is an eligibility criterion which must be met before you can qualify for a paid subscription account.

Your account needs to be in good standing (no strikes and no videos which have been blocked), it needs to meet the YouTube partnership criteria and it needs to be verified by phone. You also need an AdSense account (linked to your YouTube account) and at least 10,000 active subscribers to your channel. Furthermore, there is a list of specific countries in which the paid subscriptions feature is available.

Content ID Appeals

If a certain video of yours has been misidentified by YouTube's Content ID system, then you can choose to dispute this identification. This only works if your account is at least 30 days old.

Unlisted or Private Videos

This allows you to change the visibility of your videos. YouTube, by default, makes all uploaded videos public, which means that anyone can view them. However, you can choose to make them private or unlisted if you want, which means that only you or certain specified people will be able to view it.

Live Events

This is a very popular feature and it lets you create events, which you can stream live. Again, your account needs to be in good standing for this feature to work.

Hangouts on Air

Since Google+ and YouTube are linked through your account, you have the option of live streaming your Hangout (a feature on Google+) on your YouTube channel.

CHAPTER 3

Making Videos

What are the Functions of a YouTube Video?

The eminence of YouTube has no doubt reached unprecedented heights. The number of people who use the website each day to watch videos is roughly 4 billion and this figure continues to grow every year. People from all over the world are beginning to upload videos of their own on the website and some people have even managed to become huge celebrities in the process of showing off their skills.

So, the function of a YouTube video has ascended from simply showing your latest escapades, to becoming a statement of who you are and what you stand for. After all, what better way to express yourself than to sing, dance, act or simply share your thoughts on the biggest online video platform in the world?

People use YouTube for creating video blogs

The concept of a blog is prevalent among those who need a means to express themselves through writing. It allows you to keep track of your thoughts and see the evolution of your perception. However, not all people have the innate ability to appreciate the written word. These people would rather watch a video of the blogger talking about himself. When it is on YouTube, the blog is not just for an exclusive group of like-minded people; it is there for the entire world to see and appreciate.

Although blogging is a major function of a YouTube video, some people want to have themselves noticed. They want to stand out from the crowd, and some even have the desire to become famous. Lately, a lot of YouTube users have started posting videos of themselves singing, acting and dancing, in the hope that record companies, famous artists, actors and produces will notice them, and give them a long awaited chance.

In the academic circles, people have found their own way of using YouTube. Universities and schools continue to upload videos of lectures, tutorials and demonstrations for the benefit of students. Corporations and large companies have used YouTube as a tool for marketing their products. They stream advertisements and promotions before many YouTube videos.

So, because there is no limit to your imagination, there is no limit to what you can convey through your YouTube video. It is yours and yours entirely, so express yourself any way you choose. If people like what you say, you could even make some money through your videos!

There are certain restrictions you should be aware of though. At first, you will not be able to upload videos longer than 15 minutes. You do have the ability to increase this limit and you will be asked to provide verification through your mobile phone. Secondly, there are age related restrictions on the type of content that you upload. Avoid using vulgar (sexually explicit or profane) language in your videos, as this is not appropriate for younger viewers.

Avoid depicting graphic and disturbing imagery, such as intense

violence. YouTube delineates that journalists and documentarians are increasingly using the website for uploading their videos and some of these can be quite graphic. So, if your video does contain strong imagery, be sure to use the description section to explain to viewers exactly what the video is about, in order to avoid confusion and alarm.

Finally, do not upload videos with nudity, sexually suggestive content or dangerous activities being performed, as these can all send the wrong messages to viewers.

How to Make a Video for YouTube

So how do become a part of YouTube, after all? Well, we have already looked at creating a YouTube account, which is the first step, but what you really need to do to become a part of the YouTube community, is to create and upload your own videos and here is how you do it.

Step 1: Get Some Good Ideas

As you may already know, there are countless types of YouTube videos out there. Everything from cuddly pets like cats and dogs playing with their owners, to reviews of the latest action-packed films and video games, has been uploaded on the website by its every loyal and ever growing user base. You will see comedy clips, blooper reels, music videos and sometimes even entire feature films uploaded by users. Thus, YouTube has become a platform for people to express their creativity, their hopes and dreams, what they hold dear to them, what tickles them, what thrills them, and what makes them dance!

So, when it comes to your YouTube video, it goes without saying that the possibilities are endless. You can make a video about whatever you want to. Think about what you are hoping to accomplish by posting it on the website and the ideas will come to you!

Step 2: Record Your Video

Once you have decided what type of video you want to make, you can start planning how you will record it. Obviously, the type of video you are planning to make will dictate the type of equipment and software you will need to record it. For instance, if you want to upload a computer simulated animation, then you will need highly sophisticated computer software and a state-of-the-art animation equipment.

If, on the other hand, you want to go with a simple homemade video, like a recipe for a dish or a movie review, then all you will really need is your own camera and a means to transfer the video from the camera to your computer. Make sure you pay attention to the types of software which can be used with your camera and your current operating system (Mac OS X or Windows). All you really need to do then, is to record yourself (or someone else), and your video is made.

Step 3: Edit Your Video

This is a very important step. After you have made your video, you cannot just simply put it on YouTube. You need to make sure that it is visually and aesthetically pleasing, and is suitable for the general audience.

Although there are several types of software that can be used for this purpose, which you can install on your computer, you can also use the numerous online video editors that are available. They allow you to merge and remove video segments, adjust the audio and video quality, and add some style and flare to your video. If you are unfamiliar with video editing, countless blogs and tutorials take you through the systematic process.

Step 4: Upload Your Video

The final step after editing your video is to upload it on YouTube. You need to sign in to your account and click on the Upload button. After that, you will be taken through a series of steps, which will ask for the details of the video and will also allow you to adjust certain settings related to comments, annotations and captions. These are all optional though. Once you have gone through this process, your video will have been uploaded on YouTube.

Uploads   Date added (newest · oldest) ▼   ▦   ☰

No videos yet!

⊕ Upload a video

Types of YouTube Videos

We have already seen how there are innumerable types of YouTube videos which you can create and upload. You are free to upload any video which expresses your imagination. However, we also know that businesses are beginning to use YouTube as a platform for promoting their products and company culture.

With the ever-growing YouTube user base, this step seems only logical, and YouTube has now begun showing advertisements and promotions before its actual video clips. Therefore, for all businesses out there that are looking to make an impact through YouTube, there are several video ideas which you could use, that would really draw attention towards you. In this section, we discuss the major types of these business videos.

Product Promotional Videos

These are perhaps the most common type of business videos that you can make. They are usually quite short (2 to 3 minutes), and describe a certain product or service of yours and all the amazing benefits it provides. Making a product promotion is usually the easiest of all business videos, since most of the content will contain details of the product. You should have a strong script for the video, with interesting and informative dialogue. Pay close attention to the visual effects and do not forget the audience you are attracting through the video.

Employee Motivation Video

This is another very common type of business video, and the general content includes comments and testimonials from dedicated employees and managers who work for the company. They talk about the opportunities and benefits the company has given them and how working for the company has made their life better. This type of video may also boost the morale of those who currently work for the company. Again, you need to make sure that the dialogue sounds sincere and flawless, so that the company culture and ethics are both reflected properly in the video.

Message from the Executive

The boss is the head of all the company's activities and embodies the principles of the company. Therefore, a video message from the company executive can really make an impact on viewers. The content for the video may be anything from a product promotion to a general description about the company, but like most business videos, it needs to be very well thought-out.

Rather than simply showing the executive in his office, delivering a message, you could show him walking around various departments of

A message from an executive can make quite an impact

the company, talking about how each is integral to the smooth running of the business. He could also talk about company values and culture, and how the world benefits from their products.

Corporate Comedy

Humor leaves a longer impression on people than a serious, business oriented message. So consider adding a humorous touch to your business videos to make the audience feel more relaxed, and to make your company culture seem pleasing. Use it in the right places and in the right way, and it will show an interesting side of your business which the outside world rarely ever gets to see.

Adding Quality Content

You could simply be thinking about putting a video on YouTube or maybe, you are looking to gain some personal satisfaction by watching the numbers roll on the view counter next to your video. If you belong to the latter, then there are things, which you should be aware of before you set out to make your own YouTube video.

There are certain genres on the website, which have gained far more attention than others. According to a survey, only 30% of all videos uploaded on YouTube make up nearly 70% of all videos watched on the website. Thus, if you are looking to make yourself popular through your videos, try making one, which fits into one of the following genres:

Music Videos

This is hands-down the most popular type of video uploaded on YouTube. Although the idea behind the website is that you make your

own videos and share them, today, most music artists have created their own YouTube channels and are using them to market their latest songs. Singers such as Justin Bieber, Miley Cyrus, Taylor Swift and Lady Gaga, all have videos, which have hit millions in views. So, if you are really looking to make an impact, try uploading a good music video.

Children and Babies

The popularity of 'Charlie bit my finger' is unquestioned. In 2007, this video which showed a young boy, Harry, playing with his little brother, Charlie, who bites his finger, garnered global fame. Why? Well, primarily because we have always been fascinated with the escapades of little children. We enjoy everything about them, particularly how original they are!

Incredible Talents

We live in an amazing world and the people in it never seize to amaze us. YouTube has become a means for anyone with a talent to express themselves and show off their skills. We have seen a small boy playing an electric guitar like Jimi Hendrix, a young boy from Taiwan singing Whitney Houston's 'I Will Always Love You' and wowing the audience, and a four-year-old child prodigy playing the violin. There is no shortage of talent out there and one sure-fire way of getting your video viewed is to display your talents.

Comedy

YouTube has always been an escape route for those looking to get away from their troubles. That is primarily because there is an infinite number of videos on the website, which make you, laugh out loud. From bloopers on game shows, news reports and infomercials, to the tickling antics of children and animals, YouTube has a stockpile of comedy videos to make you laugh. Homemade videos are considered the most popular out of all of these and if you really want a huge audience, try making one yourself!

Pets and Animals

Videos of pets and animals are likely to go viral incredibly fast. Much as with children, the antics of dogs, cats, hamsters, birds and even animals in the zoo never fail to intrigue us. Cute and cuddly animals such as kittens and puppies get instant likes and YouTube users have a soft spot for their innocent, loveable tricks.

10 YouTube Video Tips

As an amateur YouTube video creator, there are certain tips you could use to make your video gain likes and views faster, and in this chapter, we have discussed some of them.

1. Content is Vital

The first step in creating a YouTube video is also the most important for ensuring its popularity. You need to have content and ideas which will attract viewers not just from a specific clique, but from all walks of life. The video needs to be informative, entertaining and engaging at the same time. That is the only way it will go viral.

2. Success Depends on How You Measure It

What you call success may be significantly different from what others call success on YouTube. Your goal should be in your mind when you create and upload your videos. Whether it is garnering 10 likes or 10,000, you need to define your own criteria for a successful YouTube video.

3. Use a Good Camera

If you are seriously considering uploading a YouTube video, then it may be worth investing in a good video camera. It goes without saying that for the general viewer, video quality is one of the most important things about a YouTube video. Without it, you could have a solid story to share, but you will get nowhere. There are countless choices for cameras out there, so pick a good one.

4. Use Closed-Caption in Your Videos

You may think that tags and annotations will work just fine, but there is nothing that beats closed-captioning! Using it will give your video a more professional and accessible look, and will clarify any dialogue that the viewer does not fully understand through the audio alone.

5. Use Appropriate Lighting

This is very important if you are thinking about doing a product promotion or review. The viewers need to be able to clearly see what you ware showing them, and although you will not necessarily need stage lighting, it is worthwhile to have enough light to allow any details in your video to be clearly visible.

6. Let Yourself Speak!

Not everyone has the confidence to produce a good YouTube video. You, however, have discovered that you do! So find the voice inside yourself and allow it to speak out. If you are very enthusiastic about something, make sure people get the message. That is the best way to enjoy making a YouTube video and to enjoy the success that comes with it.

7. Be Original nor not

The whole point of a YouTube video is that you allow yourself to express who YOU are. So do not try to be someone you are not, because your viewers will get that immediately, and you may be labelled as fake. Be original, with all your quirks and foibles, and people will love you for it.

8. Create a URL Playlist

If you are looking to promote several videos, then creating a playlist of video URLs can significantly improve the experience of the viewer. Closely related videos are played automatically one after another, and your viewers will stay interested.

9. Practice

Although you may have a great video idea, it is worthwhile to compose clips and segments a few times before you upload the actual video on YouTube. Have your friends view it and ask for their honest opinion. Record multiple segments and watch them closely for what you like and do not like. Then, you can improve.

10. Be Humorous

Humor is a very powerful tool when it comes to creating a pleasing user experience. Practice timing your jokes perfectly so that they are understood by the viewers. However, do not overdo it because it can distract the viewers (and yourself even) from the true purpose of your video.

Make Your Videos Go Viral

Promote Your Videos

In order for you to really make your YouTube video reach the masses, you need to promote it any way you can. These strategies are particularly useful if you are a small or medium business looking to market your products or services through recently uploaded videos.

1. Use YouTube to its fullest. This means that you should use any features the website offers to make your videos complete and to make them stand out. Give them a good, appropriate title along with a detailed description of what they are about. Be sure to use tags and keywords.
2. Use a call-to-action to allow users to comment on your videos, rate them, like them and even share them on their own channels. This way your videos will gradually spread.
3. Spread your videos in your own circle. Promote them among your friends, acquaintances and clients, and get their feedback. Then ask them to like them and share them with other people.
4. Use social networking sites to your advantage. Nearly everyone has a Facebook, LinkedIn, Google+, MySpace or Twitter account. Post your videos on them. People will like them and comment on them. Those who really like them may share them on their own profiles as well.
5. Share your videos on your own company website. Include them in blogs and link them to any products and services you are offering, so that your clients can get a better idea about them.
6. Share your videos with your current clientele via email (or any other means).

7. Get in touch with bloggers, editors and reporters through press releases and public relations techniques, and hire them to generate media coverage for your videos. This is an excellent way to make your videos reach your intended audience.

8. Search engines are the most powerful tools on the internet these days. Make sure your videos are listed with major search engines such as Google, Yahoo and Bing. You could also post them on LinkedIn and Pinterest if you think it is appropriate. Give them keyword-associated names, so that they show up on popular searches, and get your YouTube channel listed as well.

9. Collaborate with other companies that are using YouTube to attract the same type of audience as you. Obviously, they should not be in competition with you. This will allow you to attract clients who already subscribe to these companies' channels and videos.

10. If your company produces printed material such as catalogues, brochures and magazines, start incorporating content from your videos in these. Also, incorporate them in your regular advertising campaign.

11. Consider hiring a marketing company, which works specifically with YouTube videos, in order to help you promote your videos through an online promotional campaign.

Use Tags and Keywords

In order for you to really make your videos go viral, you need to do Search Engine Optimization (SEO). This is crucial whether you are an individual, looking to spread your YouTube videos to the masses, or particularly if you are a small to medium sized business, looking to promote your products and services through your videos.

The use of search engines, to promote your videos, has already been stressed in the previous chapter. If your videos get many hits with search engines such as Google, Yahoo! and Bing, then you can be sure that they will reach all interested viewers.

YouTube is the largest online video search engine, and Google is the largest search engine. So, if you want your clients to be able to find your videos, then using both of them properly is crucial. The only ways in which search engines identify a video as being relevant to a particular search are through the metadata (description of the video content) and the closed-caption description of the video.

Using SEO for your videos is nearly the same as using SEO for your website content. You should be aware of what keywords and phrases should be used i.e. ones that you think people will search for when they are trying to find relevant videos. You should use these in your video titles and descriptions.

Outside the content, the title is perhaps the most important part of the video. That is because it is the first place that people will look for when they are performing a search. So, use a keyword or phrase in the title of your video.

Next is the description. Like metadata for websites and articles, the description of your video will appear on searches performed with Google and YouTube. Therefore, it is a good idea to include keywords throughout the description, particularly in the first two or three lines. If the video does not contain easily identifiable information about the organization, brand name, or a certain person, then these should be included in the description as well.

YouTube allows users to add tags to the descriptions of their videos. As opposed to keywords, which may be long phrases that you can include in the video description, tags are single words which YouTube allows you to add, in order for searches to sort out and filter videos.

Again, you should try to add tags that focus on things that are not easily identifiable through the content of the video, but which you think are important. They could be generic, but that might not be very helpful for YouTube searches. Having tags that focus on specific things will make it easier for others to find your videos. Using tags also allows YouTube to categorize your video into one of its 15 major categories.

Good Video Quality

YouTube viewers find it very easy to tell amateur video makers apart from professional, dedicated ones. When you search for something on the website, you will find poor quality videos, where the details are barely visible and the sound is awful. Then there are those which are slightly better, with average video quality and sound, but still lacking in something.

Finally, there are the best YouTube videos, made by the professionals. These have immaculate video quality and sound, and are definitely the most watched. Therefore, if you really want your videos to gain likes and views, and you are dedicated to your work, you need to focus on the quality of your video.

The first and most important thing is to get yourself a good camera. This is essential if you want professional looking results, and there are numerous types of digital video cameras available in the market these days. Some of these are HD (High Definition), and are certainly worth an investment. Try to get one with a 1080p HD video mode, as this is the best mode for YouTube videos.

After the video quality, sound becomes the second most important thing for any YouTube video, so focus on it as well. Viewers will not be interested in a video where nothing is audible, or everything is too loud! Try not to use the microphone on the camera itself, because this does not give good sound. Instead, you could try using an external microphone, which is far more convenient.

Try to stabilize your video camera while you are filming. Unless used very skillfully, shaky video will not make your efforts seem dedicated and professional. Therefore, you should try to use any equipment, which will stabilize your camera and improve the quality of your video. A tripod stand is perhaps the best way to do this, but you can also use a device such as a steady-cam.

Improve your general skill as a videographer, but studying and learning advanced filming techniques. There are countless websites and tutorials

available on the internet, which will cover topics such as lighting, positioning, orientation, focus, composure and framing. Generally, try not to keep the subject of your shot in the center of the video, as this will decrease the shot quality. Also, pay close attention to objects in the foreground and background, and use them to your advantage if you can.

Use video editing software to give your videos the touches that will make them look professional. These software give you a lot of control over effects, lighting, background and animations, so do use them to keep the viewers interested. A detailed description of video editing is given in the next chapter.

Finally, keep practicing making videos. As with any activity which demands skill and patience, eventually you will get better, and you will make your YouTube videos much more interesting.

Edit Your Videos

Editing is a very important step in making a video, and one that most amateur video makers often neglect. You should use both the hardware and software you have at your disposal to give your videos final touches in order to make them more professional. In this chapter, we will look at the steps you should follow when editing your videos.

Use editing techniques to enhance your videos

The first thing to do is to transfer your captured video from your camera to a computer. These days most digital cameras come with their USB cable, so this should not be too difficult. Transfer them to a secure location, so that they do not accidentally get deleted and pay attention to their file format.

Then start viewing the footage which you have recorded, and create a log/record. This will allow you to identify which segments you want to keep, which ones you want to edit, and which you want to remove completely. Then, open your editing software. There are several available, and some of the popular ones include Windows Movie Maker, Final Cut Pro, Avidemux and YouTube Vide Editor (which is available online).

Start a new project in the video editor. You should also have learnt to capably use your video editing software. The three main elements of your video editing software are the timeline options, the preview window and the video library.

The timeline allows you to organize the sequence of your segments. The preview window lets you analyse the changes and effects, which have been added to your chosen segment. The video library lets you view the various media files which have been imported into your video editor.

Start by importing a video into your project. The library will allow you to see which files are available to be imported. Once imported, the video will play in the timeline section, and you can slice it into different segments, as per your preferences. After slicing, the various segments can be arranged in any order you want. This is the whole point of editing in the timeline section.

If you play the video in the timeline section, then it should appear in the preview window as well. Some software have scrubbers which you can drag back and forth to play your selected video one frame at a time. By now, even if you were a novice at video editing, you should have developed some idea of how to go about it.

So, here is your chance to play around. Use the preview window to add effects to improve your video quality. Move segments back and forth, patch them together, and do whatever you feel will make the video more entertaining and interesting!

The more you use your video editing software, the better you will get at it. Once you are finished, play the video one final time for yourself, and also let your friends watch it. Ask for their comments and edit your video again if necessary. If not, then you are ready to upload it on YouTube!

Steer Clear of Inappropriate Content

You need to be very careful when uploading your videos on YouTube. If you have used YouTube before and browed the videos extensively, then you may think that any type of video can be uploaded, but this is not at all true. There are very strict guidelines on the content of a video, which you must follow. You must not post videos:

- which are pornographic in nature, or are sexually explicit
- which contain nudity of any sort
- which are extremely violent, or contain graphic imagery
- which contain extremely disturbing or disgusting content
- which violate any sort of copyright laws
- which contain hateful material, particularly verbal, against a certain gender, sexual preference, race, ethnic background, religion, disability, political orientation or nationality
- which reveal personal information about a person, particularly a YouTube user

YouTube employees or staff do not directly enforce these guidelines. This is because there are on average approximately 65,000 new videos being uploaded every single day on the website. This makes it nearly impossible for them to browse each one.

Therefore, the actual enforcing and reporting is carried out by other YouTube users. A very strong user community is the backbone of how all videos are made according to YouTube guidelines.

If a user finds a video, which is inappropriate, or violates the guidelines in any way, it can be reported immediately using the 'flag' button next to it. This alerts the staff who can then take a look at it. If the video is found to contain disagreeable content, then it is removed from the website, and a warning is sent to the user who uploaded it. In some serious cases the users account may also be deleted.

So unless you want to be permanently banned from YouTube, be very careful when uploading your videos. Make sure they adhere to the guidelines, and do not contain any inappropriate material.

CHAPTER 4

Make Yourself Famous on YouTube

Brand Yourself

Have you ever advertised your product or brand on YouTube? If yes, how? A virtual presence is important, but at times, it takes a lot more to brand yourself on the internet. What do you understand by the phrase "brand yourself?" Have you ever given it a thought?

An impressive logo or a catchy tag line is never a guarantee for success. What makes a YouTube channel so appealing and attractive? More importantly, how do you create traffic and increase viewer engagement?

If you want to advertise your product on YouTube, follow the below stated steps:

Design a Customized Avatar

An avatar is like an emblem, which signifies your brand and is associated with any form of activity related to your brand. Whenever someone likes, comments, posts or subscribes to your brand, the avatar would pop up in front of them. Therefore, an avatar attracts people towards it, generating a high number of likes, traffic and comments. Make sure you design an avatar which is eye catching, appealing and attractive, at the same time.

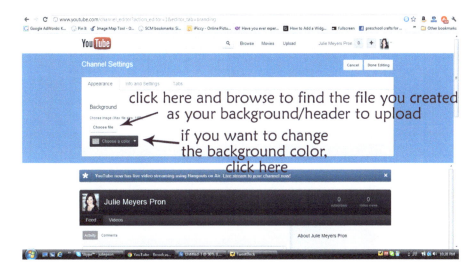

Include Your Channel Name

Your channel name is perhaps the next, most important thing, after, of course, your brand name. Make sure your channel name is visible and prominent; it should be mentioned in the first few seconds of your videos. Since your channel name helps you develop a deep-rooted association with it, make sure you increase its recall and recognition.

Integrate Social Media

Always make sure that you advertise your social media web pages, alongside your YouTube page. Social media integration is of the utmost importance, especially when it comes to branding yourself. Try to include a brief description of your business, so that people know what you stand for.

SEO

As part of your Search Engine Optimization, whenever you upload a video, make sure you add descriptions and tags. In this way, it would become more visible on various search engines. Moreover, make sure you include a brand tag, which would not only promise you effective search-ability, but would also help in forming a thread of "related videos." In this way, whenever viewers tune to other channels, they can automatically be redirected towards yours, if there is a common brand tag.

Add a Video Bumper

A brand bumper is a basic depiction of your channel's logo and name. Make sure you insert a 5 second video bumper, at the start of your video. However, keep them short and sweet, or else you might come off as too "sales-y."

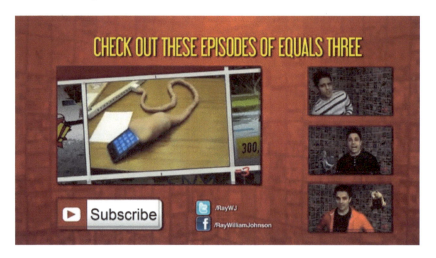

Include an End Slate

After watching a video, you will see an array of other related videos on the same screen. Make sure you add your logo in the background, so that on some level of consciousness, the logo and name of your brand remains alive and fresh in the viewer's minds.

Optimize Your Channel

Today's golden era is all about effective communication and the role social media plays in the development of communication channels is phenomenal. So much so, almost 96% of small businesses in the US have some form of presence on social media.

Similarly, many people emphasize on the importance of having a separate YouTube channel; little do they know that their responsibility does not only end here. You need to make your YouTube channel prominent and visible in search engines, a process which is known as search engine optimization. Keep the following tips in mind, if you want to optimize your channel:

Quality Content

The first and foremost rule of maintaining a YouTube channel is to develop quality content. Many companies hire specialist digital agencies to manage their social media forums. Before writing content for your channel, make sure you conduct a keyword search or a content analysis search. This would inform you about viewer insights and would indicate exactly what they are looking for.

Moreover, keep your competitors in the loop and try to figure out the keywords they are paying the most emphasis on. Lastly, remember that amongst the clutter on the internet, you only have a few seconds to capture the viewer's attention. Make your content such that it engages, excites and interests your viewer, within those crucial initial seconds.

Make an Optimized Title

Since YouTube is known as the second largest social network in the world, make sure your video title is SEO friendly and includes suitable keywords. Having the right keywords would not only facilitate search results on YouTube, it would also guarantee visibility on other search engines. Make sure you keep the following in mind:

- Your video title should not be more than 66 characters
- The name of your brand should be mentioned at the end
- Try to incorporate the word "video" in your title, so that it aids search-ability
- Try to pilot test video titles and gauge their relative popularity

Optimize Your Video Tags

Video tags are another way to ensure your search engine optimization. They allow you to be positioned in organic searches. Therefore, make sure your video tags contain such words which can be readily searched, even in other search engines. Choose your video tags wisely, since they determine the rating of your video in respective search engines, or under the "related content" column.

Make Logical Annotations

Annotations refer to the process of linking and relating various videos to a series of related videos, or to a related brand. Annotations enable a user to stick to one page, for at least a few minutes, by engaging and redirecting him to other social media links. You can utilize the time that the user is on your page, simply by encouraging signups and registrations. Therefore, make sure you put considerable time and effort in designing your annotations.

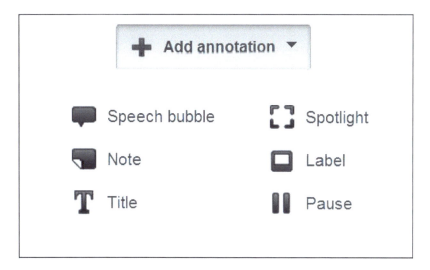

Transcribe Your Videos

If you think you lack the resources to conduct a full-fledged research on finding out the right way to caption your videos, try transcribing them. It is always advisable to propose a script for your video and to upload it. Search engines would automatically try to index captions, according to their knowledge of key words and based on an understanding of the relevant script.

Therefore, always remember: developing a YouTube channel is an easier task than maintaining it.

Engaging With Your Audience

Nothing can spell disaster more than a non-interactive YouTube page. Gone are the days when having a presence on the internet was more than what was bargained for. Today's age is that of communication and interactivity. Try to engage with your audience in the most personal way possible and always remember, it is extremely hard to attract a viewer, but even harder to retain one.

Engaging with your audience is the most important element of social media marketing and large multinationals are spending millions just to develop a personal network with its users. Therefore, try to engage with your audience in the following way:

Always Know What They Want

You should know what your viewers are interested in, which topics would they like to talk about and, above all, what type of videos would they be interested in. If you wish to gain invaluable insights related to the viewer's likes and dislikes, follow their comments, complaints and opinions on your and your competitor's videos and other social media forums.

Avoid Robotic Replies

The first and most important rule of engagement is to personalize your communication efforts and to interact with your audience on the same wavelength. Simply sending a robotic reply is a waste of time. Talk to your audience as if you are interacting with them face-to-face. Speak as if you are actually speaking to them, listen as if that is the only thing you want to do and respond as if you have all the time in the world.

Make Good Titles

Amongst the clutter already present on the internet, how do you make sure you stand out? Poor titles encourage passer-bys, while catchy and interactive ones encourage visitors, it is as simple as that. Therefore, always do your research and make your titles as relevant to current trends, as possible.

Do Not Try to be Someone You Are Not

The entire point of a YouTube channel is to put forth your product and point of view. Therefore, always try to be as original as possible and try to offer the audience something different, a unique selling point, perhaps, which would help you stand out from the clutter.

Always Reply to Comments

Uploading even the highest quality and interesting videos would do you no good, until and unless you make it a habit to reply to viewers' comments and queries. Make the audience feel that their input is highly valuable and that their feedback is much appreciated. Do not shy away from giving your opinion; if you want to disagree, do so politely.

Practice and implement the above points, if you wish to increase your engagement level with your audience.

Stay Relevant

If you want to be amongst the top trending channels on YouTube, you would have to earn that right. The first and foremost rule of developing a social presence in the media is to stay relevant. Add the right content, promote specific features and most importantly, communicate with your audience.

There are three essentials which you should abide by if you want to make your YouTube channel a hit amongst your target audience. If you are just a beginner, follow the guide illustrated below:

Create a Buzz

Do you want your audience to be excited and thrilled about your brand? Do you want them to anticipate each of your new releases? If yes, then creating a buzz is the most important tool of promotion. You can create a buzz around your brand in the following way:

Think Global, Act Local

Even if you are a global brand, with high international coverage, make sure your audience can relate to your videos. Research on the most trending topics and news in each geographic area, then try to revolve your promotional campaigns around that idea or concept. Translate your posts into different languages or use subtitles in different languages.

Make Parodies

Search for the most famous videos on YouTube and start commenting on them. If you want to capture the attention of your audience, create parodies of the most popular videos on YouTube. This would automatically connect your parodies to the original, famous videos.

Add Slice of Life Videos

Most advertisers have recently implemented the "slice of life" concept in their various adverts and campaigns. Revolving your video around the life of a common man would only make your audience relate to it on a greater level. The trick is to keep uploading videos and add original and interesting content, so that it attracts the viewer's attention.

Connect With Your Audience

Without a well-established connection with your viewers, you would never be able to promote your brand, in the manner you want. Therefore, connect with your audience in the following ways:

Add Tags to Your Videos

Try to come up with new, exciting and original tags for your videos and never make the mistake of uploading one without tags. Conduct a key word search and find out the most searched words on search engines. Keeping this in mind, use specific, detailed and relevant tags for your videos.

Promote Your Videos

If you have the right content and quality video, people will soon recognize and appreciate it. Use other social networking sites to propel your popularity. Facebook, Pinterest and LinkedIn are essential portals to help you succeed.

Never Compromise on Your Video Quality

Originality

Never try to be someone you are not, especially in your videos. It takes a matter of 10-15 seconds for a user to determine whether your content is original and whether you are funny or not. Treat your brand as a separate entity and attach humanistic characteristics to it. Try to pinpoint areas of strength and flaunt them in your videos.

Offer Something Unique

What are your unique selling points? Your expertise? Are they your product's features? Or your top notch service? Whatever it is, try to integrate it in your videos and offer something so unique to your audience, that they end up wanting to see more.

Collaborate with Famous YouTubers

Have you ever wondered why people get so popular, all of a sudden, on YouTube? More importantly, how do they get viral on the second largest social media forum? Starting from a single video, they make themselves into a brand and eventually make an entire channel for themselves. This applies to products, services and even people.

Some pop artists we see today were initially discovered on YouTube and their claim to fame was one, poorly shot but thoroughly exciting home video. If you want to hop on the bandwagon to success, use YouTube as a means of promotion. Rest assured, you would be surprised at the rate of clicks and hits, given that people like your video.

What are Collaborative Videos?

Do you know what collaborative videos are? Have you ever heard about them? Collaborative videos involve two people, with different YouTube accounts, sharing resources to make one collective video. In simple terms, one party sends their video clips to the other, while the other merges them to make one video. If you want fast and easy fame, might as well try to collaborate with famous YouTubers.

One of the most effective ways to promote yourself on YouTube is to collaborate with famous YouTubers. If you have several businesses, this would be a great opportunity to cross collaborate your brands. This technique offers various advantages; some of them are listed below:

Element of Personalization

Make it a point to attend YouTube gatherings, which are informal meetings held all over the world. This gives you the chance to meet famous YouTubers in person, thus allowing you to invite them personally to join your channel. Try to make connections and make them like you. After inviting them, thank them for their time and ask them if they are interested in making collaborative videos. Only if you let your personality charm them, will you be able to collaborate your efforts and come up with something completely new and exciting.

Useful for Beginners

For those of you who are new to the world of YouTube and have no prior experience or a reputation, collaborating with famous YouTubers would be the perfect way to get a kick start. This can enable you to benefit from their well established reputation and attaching your name with them might give you the "big break" you have always wanted.

Gain Recognition

Contacting famous YouTubers by meeting them in gatherings or simply by contacting them through social media, might gain you the recognition you have always wanted. However, make sure you pitch in your idea and concept well; a weak pitch is never enough to interest the other party. In this way, you can become a part of the YouTube community and share a greater chunk of viewership. What more can you ask for, especially this early in your career?

CHAPTER 5

Maximize the Potential of YouTube

The Basics of Revenue-Sharing

Have you ever wondered how to make money on YouTube? Have you ever tried to do so? It seems like a hard nut to crack, doesn't it? It might have been a difficult task previously, but the new revenue sharing program introduced by YouTube has made making money a piece of cake!

What is the Revenue-Sharing Program?

The Revenue-Sharing program allows several content owners to gain profitability by sharing a stake in the revenue generated by the ads placed in videos. However, this option was only open to the most popular content developers.

This signalled bad news for those developers who did not have much popularity over the network. Even if a video went viral, they wouldn't be able to benefit from it because they weren't enrolled in the program, in the first place. However, YouTube has recently altered its program, which now provides an opportunity to everyone to make some money, whenever they hit the jackpot, that is.

How it Works?

With the new features added to the original revenue-sharing program, the program caters to all developers who have an account on YouTube. YouTube conducts a regular assessment of the various videos that recently went viral. It then sends an email to the uploader of the videos, which acts as an invitation to join the revenue-sharing program.

After accepting the offer, YouTube will automatically attach ads against your videos, alongside giving you a share of the revenue generated from the ads. If your video has high views, it is viral and it is compatible with the Terms and Conditions, you are eligible to enroll in this program.

"The company expects to 'increase the number of partners dramatically' up into the tens of thousands of partners (up from thousands). The revenue share will be the same as what applies to the general Partnership Program, with the majority of the revenue going to the content contributor,"- Tom Pickett, Director of Online Sales and Operations at YouTube.

This program gives developers and uploaders the opportunity to make extra bucks from a viral video. The more viral your video, the greater the number of ads attached to them, thus greater the revenue. Moreover, the program is not only limited to recently viraled videos, it also incorporates older ads that were once viraled, but never really attached a monetary value to.

Therefore, if you want to make extra revenue on your most popular videos, enable the revenue-sharing tool on your YouTube account. The primary advantage of this program, especially for small developers, is that they can finance their less-popular videos with the extra revenue generated by the popular and more viral ones. So, what are you waiting for? Focus all your efforts and resources in developing a super hit video, so that you become eligible for this program. Once you become part of it, the ads attached to the videos also act as redirecting tool for your YouTube channel.

How to Become a YouTube Partner

Do you have a channel on YouTube? Have you uploaded any videos on it? Are any of the videos generating views, reviews or comments? Are people subscribing to your channel on a daily basis? If yes, you should probably start making money off these videos.

Have you ever heard of the YouTube Partnership Program? If not, then you should probably start thinking about enrolling yourself into it. This particular program not only gives you an opportunity to generate extra revenue, it also expands your viewership.

If you are interested in becoming a YouTube partner, follow the steps stated below:

Develop a Basic Understanding of the Partner's Program

Before you delve into the Partnership Program, you should develop a basic understanding of how it actually works. The process is quite simple. Ads are attached to your most popular videos and you get a proportion of revenue generated from those ads. As an added monetary benefit, YouTube pays you a $500 gift certificate, if you manage to attract a total of 100,000 subscribers. Those developers, who reach about a million subscribers, receive a gold plaque from Google. Such a form of monetary reward motivates various developers to join the partnership program.

The YouTube Partner Program: *Cash in on your creativity*

YouTube partners are independent video creators and media companies who are looking for online distribution and who meet our qualifications. Becoming a partner gives you the ability to share in ad revenue from your YouTube videos.

Why become a partner?

Effective Monetization
YouTube maintains a positive user experience with automatically targeted, creative ad formats that generate revenue when your videos are viewed. All you need to do is create compelling video content.

Widest Reach
Your content will be delivered to the largest worldwide online video community via YouTube and our syndication partners.

Non-Exclusive Agreement
We don't restrict where you can upload and distribute your videos.

See our current content partners

Who qualifies for partnership?
To become a partner, you need to meet these criteria.

✓ You **create original videos** suitable for online streaming.

✓ You **own the copyrights** and distribution rights for all audio and video content that you upload – no exceptions.

✓ You regularly upload videos that are **viewed by thousands** of YouTube users.

✓ You live in the **United States** or **Canada**.

Do you qualify, and want to become a partner? **Apply now**

Attach a Monetary Value to Your Videos

After receiving an email to enroll into the partnership program, you need to tweak your settings, so that your videos can be monetarily attached to various ads. However, the monetizing process does not apply to almost all your videos. Each video is first analysed and scrutinized, before ads are attached against them.

Your ads should comply with the terms and conditions of the partnership agreement. You should have rights to all components of your video, be it the music, imagery or the content. Your videos would not be monetized until and unless you have the permission or right to use everything in your video.

After joining the program, make sure you enable the monetizing procedure on all your previous ads; do not wait for them to automatically be attached to the monetizing program.

If you are wondering how you will receive regular payment from the ad revenue, your answer lies in creating an AdSense account. You need to open up an account and connect it to your YouTube account, so that it can keep track of your on-going activities.

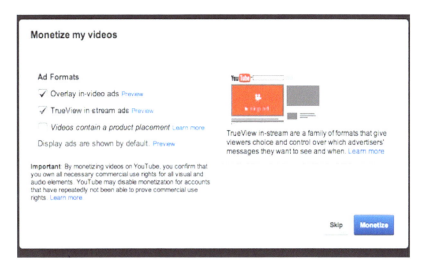

Receive Payments

When receiving ad payments, you need to follow a particular protocol. You would be required to pay a minimum tax payment and provide a payment address. An automated PIN number would be generated and assigned to your AdSense account.

For your convenience, the AdSense account has multiple currency denominations, which can be used according to your preference. However, there is a revenue criteria which needs to be fulfilled, before you can receive payments. Based on the currency you choose, the minimum amount of revenue would differ.

Make sure you abide by the following, if you want to become an active member of the Partnership Program. More and more businesses are subscribing to this new program due to the various monetary and non-monetary benefits of this program.

Partner Earnings from Advertising Revenues

The phenomenon of "making money on YouTube" has gained momentum and interest from the masses. The primary reason for its popularity is, perhaps, the weekly or monthly revenue generated by ads. This acts as a safety net for those developers who hardly make much out of their videos, all year round.

How to Partner Your YouTube Account?

Have you ever uploaded a video on YouTube? However, only a select few can actually become YouTube partners. Previously, only a few, select people were allowed to enter the program and the rest were deemed ineligible. However, this has recently changed and almost anyone with a substantial YouTube standing can become a partner.

Make sure you comply with the terms and conditions of the program, otherwise Google might have to intervene to remove the video from YouTube and take corrective measures.

"There are more than a million channels in the Partner Program (up from 30,000 in 2011), with YouTube estimated to take a 45/55 share of the ad revenue. Official figures aren't available but partners only really make a fraction of a cent per view,"- YouTube Officials.

The question remains, how to make money off YouTube? One of the most predominant ways to do so is to partner earnings from advertising revenues.

How do YouTube Partners Earn from Advertising Revenues?

YouTube earns around 45% of the total revenue generated by ads, whereas the cost per thousand (CPM) tends to vary. Various factors such as your geographic location and nature of content determines your level of earnings. On average, however, partners tend to earn around $0.3 to $2.5, while the YouTube giants earn $10 CPM. Always remember that only monetized videos promise a return. If you have an old video, which has many views, but hasn't been monetized, you will not be able to earn a dime from it. If you feel that you cannot keep track of your video ratings, there is a small calculator built in your AdSense account. This would help you calculate your earnings, depending on the CPM rates of your videos. All you need to do is make an AdSense account and connect it with your YouTube account.

Figure 15. YouTube Revenue Analysis

	2010A	2011E	2012E
Current Annualized WW Page Views (000s)	808,392	929,651	1,050,506
Y/Y Growth	20%	15%	13%
CPM	$1.02	$1.43	$1.61
Estimated YouTube Gross Revenue	**$825**	**$1,328**	**$1,695**
% of YouTube Revenue With Revenue Share	50%	50%	50%
YouTube Revenue from Monetizable Videos (MMs)	**$412**	**$664**	**$848**
Revenue Share	68%	68%	68%
Net Revenue Post Rev Share (MMs)	**$132**	**$212**	**$271**
Total Net Revenue (MMs)	**$544**	**$876**	**$1119**

Source: Citi Investment Research and Analysis; comScore

Being part of the Partnership Program involves many steps and procedures, but it is highly rewarding, especially in purely monetary terms. So, what are you waiting for? Start generating views on your YouTube videos and you would be eligible for the program in no time.

Partner Earnings from Sponsorships and Merchandise Deals

Do you know what a vlogger is? A vlogger is a blogger of videos, a term that is assigned to the users of the second largest social network, YouTube. YouTube allows you to be more than just a vlogger, it promises you a profit-sharing role in its advertising revenue. If you wish to make easy bucks off of your content, roll up your sleeves and get started.

After partnering your YouTube account with the Partnership Program, you might start thinking of getting hold of high-end sponsorships or merchandize deals. Here, you will have to think fast and act smart. Follow the step-by-step guide given below before venturing into any kind of sponsorship deal.

Steps to Get Sponsorship on YouTube

1. Before you even think of getting a sponsorship, work on solidifying and expanding your existing subscriber base. As

a rule of thumb, the greater your subscribers, the more the chances of getting a sponsorship. Therefore, work on uploading quality content and engage with your audience at the same time. This has the potential of doing wonders for you and getting your YouTube channel lucrative sponsorships.

2. It is advisable to maintain a separate business email for your YouTube account especially if you have multiple businesses or ventures. This would help you stay focused, professional and, more importantly, it will help you entertain queries and concerns of various sponsors. Make sure you connect your business email to your channel.

3. Never upload controversial content on your channel. Nothing puts off a sponsor more than irrelevant and unacceptable content. Therefore, before you begin to shoot anything, make sure it complies with YouTube terms and conditions.

4. Do not perform any such act, which might force YouTube to take regulatory action against you. Do not entertain unwanted comments and do not post copyrighted material under your own label. YouTube may cancel your account and put your partnership agreement to a halt. This would tarnish the image of your brand and no sane sponsor would be willing to invest in your channel.

5. Make sure you build a rapport with video sponsors. Inform them of your brand, what you stand for and the basic aim of your channel, through letters and emails. You should also inform them about your existing subscription base, your plans for future growth and the number of daily views. Search for the major players in the industry, the ones who have a well established reputation and a strong financial backing.

A Word of Caution

Make sure you maintain strong relationships with all the members of the community and act as an active member. Keep your eyes and ears open; opportunities do not knock twice! Try to promote other channels, as a gesture of goodwill, so that the effort can be reciprocated. Connect and engage with your audience, so that you gain greater subscriptions, views and comments. In the world of YouTube, it is all about getting quality content out there and making sure it is seen, acknowledged and appreciated by people. Moreover, keep a watch out for your competitors; see what tactics they are using and how they are attracting more and more subscribers on a daily basis.

Partner Earnings from Paid Channel Subscriptions

Are you aware of what paid channels are? Have you ever maintained one, or simply come across one? The second largest social media offers another way to make money from subscriptions. With several channels getting massive views and subscriptions, the avenues to make money on YouTube grew and so did paid channels.

What is a Paid Channel?

Amongst the plethora of famous YouTube channels, a few of them are allowed to charge their users a subscription fee of 99 cents, on a monthly basis. These channels provide a two-week free trial and various discounts to those who subscribe for a yearly period. According to the YouTube rules and regulations, any channel with above 10,000 subscribers can have a paid channel. The subscription rates, on the contrary, would be arbitrarily determined, with YouTube having the final say.

"This is just the beginning," YouTube said in the blog post. "We'll be rolling paid channels out more broadly in the coming weeks as a self-service feature for qualifying partners."

How it Works

Through the YouTube Partnership Program, many channels are making money from the advertising revenue. However, paid channel subscriptions are an added means of making money, given that they are popular enough on YouTube and people are willing to pay extra to watch their channel. The paid subscription program works in a similar pattern as the partnership program, with the channel owners keeping the lion's share of the subscription fee.

Although there are not any official revelations of the revenue split between YouTube and channel owners, a rough estimate portrays that 55% of the revenue channels out to owners, while only 45% of it is retained by YouTube.

YouTube's primary aim is to divert its audience from TV and hook them onto its various channels. In pursuit of the above stated aim, the second largest social media forum has invested a total of $300 million on the production and implementation of over a 100 channels, in two years. It also has a chain of studios for its channel owners located in Los Angeles, London and Tokyo, with the fourth one under way.

How to Subscribe to a Paid Channel?

If you have more than 100,000 subscriptions, you are eligible to open up your very own paid channel. Here's how you can subscribe to one:

1. In order to subscribe to the paid channel, simply click on the "Start Free Trial" button, as illustrated below:

2. The next step involves determining whether a particular channel would show ads with its videos. You need to know if you will be able to watch what you are paying for without ads. If you look closely, in the above illustration, there is a "no advertising" post written above "start free trial" button. All the channels are quite upfront about this feature and you can choose whether you want ads or not.
3. After clicking on the start free trial button, a window such as the one illustrated below would pop up. Follow the step-by-step procedure until you finish your purchase.

4. After all the necessary information is provided, your purchase would be complete. The new channel would be added to your YouTube Guide on the left side of your page, as illustrated below.

Some subscriptions allow you to access multiple channels for an annual or monthly subscription fee. Make sure you determine whether the liberty to choose from a variety of channels is offered. Rest assured, you will not be charged twice if you have the luxury of watching multiple channels under one subscription.

How to Unsubscribe from a Paid Channel?

If you want to unsubscribe from a particular paid channel, simply click on the "unsubscribe" button located on your channel page. If your subscription includes multiple channels, you will have to remove them from your Guide. Rest assured, your other channels would remain subscribed, until you choose to unsubscribe from them.

Unsubscribing from a YouTube channel would allow you to view all videos till the billing period but if you want to access more, you will have to subscribe all over again. If you want to keep a regular check on your subscriptions, you can check the status of your channels by visiting youtube.com/purchases.

CHAPTER 6

Increase Earnings with MCNs

Do you know what MCNs are? Have you ever had a channel on YouTube? Even if you have the faintest idea of how to use YouTube, you would probably know what MCNs are. Over the years, since its inception, YouTube has grown and expanded by leaps and bounds.

What are MCNs?

MCNs, or Multiple Channel Networks, are organizations, which are external to YouTube but help in tasks such as cross-promotion, funding, product programming, audience development, sales and monetization. Since they are external entities, they are not formally affiliated with Google or YouTube. As the number of channels grew on YouTube, MCNs started to divide and conquer. MCNs sign contracts with various channels and offer their legal services in return for a cut in their advertising revenue. For the sake of variation, they are also known as Online Video Studios or YouTube Networks.

Benefits

Since MCNs are experts in the field of production, editing and programming, they can offer your channel the best support services, which can improve the quality of your videos by tenfold. This improved quality would lead to increased CPMs, a greater number of viral videos and an expanded subscription base. They can also give various YouTube channels an opportunity to make money from copyrighted cover songs of several original ones.

Apart from the listed tasks performed by MNCs, they also carry out monetization, tracking and blocking policies. Monetization enables videos to be attached against various ads and provides various avenues of revenue for channel owners and MCNs alike. MCNs can also block certain videos in various countries or geographic locations. They can also track the number of times a video has been re-uploaded or to assess any copy righted material there is.

Earnings with MCNs

Since MCNs are experts and provide professional services, they are in a better position to bargain for higher advertising rates and greater promotional packages. Due to professional packaging, sponsorships and direct sales, MCNs can exercise greater control when it comes to negotiating rates.

The earnings you gain by signing up with an MCN might not be too much, but the services it offers can often do wonders for your channel. MCNs provide you with the support you need in order to build your channel and take it to heights of success and fame.

A stronger channel is usually a guarantee of increased earnings. MCNs will offer you all the auxiliary services you need, but with the promise of a cut in your advertising revenue. If you think of this as an investment, it has the potential of generating all-time-high earnings for you in the future.

The choice is truly yours: whether you want to share your current advertising revenue for a stronger channel in the future, or would you rather reap all the revenue of your ads, with a poorly structured YouTube channel. Whichever option you choose, make sure you weigh its pros and cons. Once you sign a contract with an MCN, you will have to legally abide by it. Lastly, make sure your decision is aligned to the aims and objectives of your channel. After all, everyone wants their channel to grow and prosper, don't they?

CHAPTER 7

Create an AdSense account?

To sign up for an AdSense account through YouTube, follow the steps below:

1. Make sure your YouTube account is enabled for monetization.

Enable your channel for monetization

To check your channel's eligibility and opt in:

1. Visit the Monetization tab in your account settings.
2. If your account is in good standing and hasn't been previously disabled for monetization, click **Enable My Account**.
3. Follow the steps to accept the YouTube Monetization agreement.

You may see a different message if your your account is not enabled for monetization.

Monetize your videos

You may enable eligible videos to earn money from relevant ads after you opt in your channel for monetization. This guide (https://support.google.com/youtube/topic/1322133) has more information about how you can enable monetization for specific videos.

To be considered a YouTube partner and access promotional and skill-building opportunities, you must have at least one video approved for monetization.

Note: you may have applied for partnership but it's not required anymore unless you live in Turkey, Russia, Italy or Ukraine.

2. Submit your application to create a new AdSense account to link with your YouTube account. Once your application has been approved, you'll see a "Host account" label on the **Home** tab of your AdSense account.
    (https://support.google.com/youtube/answer/72866)

    Google will send you a payment the month after your AdSense balance exceeds $100, assuming your YouTube and AdSense accounts are in good standing.

3. If you also have your own non-host website where you'd like to show ads, then you'll need to submit a one-time application form to tell us the URL of your site.
    (https://support.google.com/adsense/answer/2534771) You only need to complete this step if you want to monetize your own website -- you don't need to take any further action to continue to monetize your YouTube videos.

    Once your one-time application is approved, the "Host account" label will be removed from the **Home** tab of your AdSense account and you'll have access to generate the AdSense ad code you need to monetize your non-host partner website.

Follow the companies that support in this book:

GROUPGLOBAL.NET
http://groupglobal.net/
http://www.facebook.com/cybershoptoday
- Office products, home and gift accessories

Global Realty & Investment Corp
http://gric-ma.com
https://www.facebook.com/globalrealtyinvestment
- Real estate sales and service

Intergalactic Travel Authority
http://ita-travelauthority.com/
https://www.facebook.com/intergalacticauthority
- Travel agent and accomodations

Innovative Publishers Inc.
http://publishing-universe.com
https://www.facebook.com/InnovativePublishers
- Book and magazine publisher

Boston School of Real Estate Inc.
http://boston-realestateschool.com
https://www.facebook.com/Boston.RealEstateSchool
- Real estate school

Taylor Pam – Fine Art LLC
http://taylorpam.com
https://www.facebook.com/taylorpam.fineartist
- Digital, acrylic and oil paintings

Love is... https://www.facebook.com/loveis.sdwebb
- Author (Love is...) and entrepreneur

How to increase sales using Pinterest
https://www.facebook.com/sellonpinterest
- Social media marketing for businesses

How to increase sales using Facebook
https://www.facebook.com/sellonline1
- Social media marketing for businesses

Design Vendors

dsgn.io

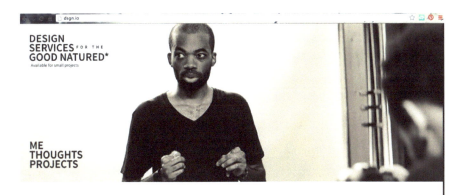

I am a proud lefty, Aries, and space bandit. The only pencil I trust is a Ticonderoga. I was born on Easter Sunday, 1988. I used to be an "Army-brat". My parents despised video games while I was growing up, so I am making up for it now (3DS, what's up?). I make music under various aliases, the most common being "the Wibby" (also FRSH∗BTS and Spaceman Fresh).

I named my portfolio "Design Services for the Good Natured" because no one likes a jerk. Every day brings about new opportunities, inspiration, and kick-ass "whoah" moments. Spread the love and do your part by inspiring others as you've been inspired! (: That's what I try to do anyway.

https://twitter.com/NetOpWibby

http://dribbble.com/nokadota

Document your progress

Title

Outcome

Start Date

Completion Date

Notes

Project Plans

Notes

Project Plans

Title

Outcome

Start Date	Completion Date

Notes

Project Plans _____

Notes

Project Plans

Title	

Outcome	

Start Date	Completion Date

Notes

Project Plans

Notes

Project Plans

Title

Outcome

Start Date	Completion Date

Notes

Project Plans

Notes

Project Plans

Title	

Outcome	

Start Date		Completion Date	

Notes

Project Plans

Notes

Project Plans

Title	

Outcome	

Start Date		Completion Date	

Notes

How to increase sales using YouTube

Project Plans

Notes

79

Project Plans

Title

Outcome

Start Date	Completion Date

Notes

Project Plans

Notes

Project Plans

Title

Outcome

Start Date

Completion Date

Notes

Project Plans

Notes

Project Plans

Title	

Outcome	

Start Date	Completion Date

Notes

Project Plans

Notes

Project Plan

Title	

Outcome	

Start Date		Completion Date	

Notes

Project Plans _____

Notes

Project Plans

Title	

Outcome	

Start Date	Completion Date

Notes

Project Plans

Notes

Project Plans

Title	
Outcome	

Start Date	Completion Date

Notes

Project Plans

Notes

Project Plans

Title

Outcome

Start Date

Completion Date

Notes

Project Plans

Notes

Project Plans

Title

Outcome

Start Date

Completion Date

Notes

Project Plans

Notes

Project Name

Title

Outcome

Start Date	Completion Date

Notes

Project Plans

Notes

Project Plans

Title

Outcome

Start Date

Completion Date

Notes

Project Plans

Notes

Project Plans

Title

Outcome

Start Date	Completion Date

Notes

Project Plans

Notes

Project Plans

Title

Outcome

Start Date

Completion Date

Notes

Project Plans

Notes

Project Plan

Title

Outcome

Start Date	Completion Date

Notes

How to increase sales using YouTube

Project Name

Title

Outcome

Start Date	Completion Date

Notes

Project Plans

Title	

Outcome	

Start Date	Completion Date

Notes

Project Plans

Notes

Project Plans

Title	

Outcome	

Start Date		Completion Date	

Notes

Project Plans

Title	
Outcome	

Start Date	Completion Date

Notes

Project Plans

Title	

Outcome	

Start Date	Completion Date

Notes

Project Plans

Notes

Project Plans

Title

Outcome

Start Date

Completion Date

Notes

How to increase sales using YouTube

Project Plans

Title	

Outcome	

Start Date	Completion Date

Notes

Project Plans

Title

Outcome

Start Date

Completion Date

Notes

Trademark Disclaimer

Product names, logos, brands and other trademarks referred to within Innovative Publishers Inc.'s publications products and services and within innovative-publishers.com are the property of their respective trademark holders. These trademark holders are not affiliated with Innovative Publishers Inc., our products, or our website. They do not sponsor or endorse our materials.

All trademarks remain property of their respective holders, and are used only to directly describe the products being provided. Their use in no way indicates any relationship between Twisted Lincoln, Inc. and the holders of said trademarks.

Innovative Publishers

Double Click Press

www.ingramcontent.com/pod-product-compliance
Lightning Source LLC
Chambersburg PA
CBHW041142050326
40689CB00001B/449